BASIC READING SERIES

WORKBOOK

LEVEL D

A King on a Swing

by Donald Rasmussen and Lynn Goldberg

BASIC READING
BERKELEY·CALIFORNIA

To Parents and Teachers

Donald Rasmussen and Lynn Goldberg developed the BASIC READING SERIES (BRS) in the early 1960s at the Miquon School, a small parent-teacher cooperative near Philadelphia. At that time, most children were taught to read using the "sight" or "look-say" method epitomized by the "Dick and Jane" readers, and many were left behind. Don and Lynn knew there must be a better way, so they spent five years developing their own reading program based on the work of the renowned linguist Leonard Bloomfield. They called their method *"inductive whole-word phonics, with a strong linguistics research base."*

After tryouts in inner-city and suburban schools around the country and almost a dozen revisions, the BASIC READING SERIES was published by Science Research Associates (SRA) and enjoyed great success. Over the years, other reading methods have come and then gone out of favor. Now, decades later, phonics is recognized as the scientific approach to reading instruction, and the BASIC READING SERIES is once again available.

BRS is divided into six levels — Levels A to F — with a reader and a workbook for each level. In Level D, children are introduced to two consonant letters that represent a single sound that is different from the sound represented by either consonant singly, such as *sh, ch, th, ng,* and *wh.* Also introduced are a 3-letter, 1-sound cluster of letters (*tch*), the ending *-ing, q* in combination with *u,* and combinations of older words with newly introduced words. In addition, 55 new exceptional words (mostly common contractions) are introduced.

The BRS Workbooks

The workbooks for BRS contain material with which children can practice their decoding skills independently of teacher direction. The decoding experiences thus provided increase the children's opportunities to discover sound-spelling relationships and to develop automatic word recognition. The workbooks are also an aid to vocabulary, word-meaning, and concept development, as they lead children to associate words with appropriate visual images and challenge children to deal with the meanings of words, phrases, and sentences. Finally, the workbooks are a useful tool with which to evaluate the children's decoding progress.

The workbook for Level D has six sections of exercises, which correspond (in their sound-spelling patterns only) to the six sections of the Level D reader, *A King on a Swing.* The exercises are not tied to the story content of the reader, however. Each section is identified by numbered tabs in the margins of its pages and begins with a word chart that presents most of the new words for that section of Level D. Each section progresses from simple exercises based on single words and phrases to more complex exercises involving phrases and sentences.

The workbook is easy to use. Children answer each item in one of three ways: by circling a word or phrase; by writing a numeral in a box; or by placing an X on a blank or in a box. Since no handwriting skill is needed, the children's reading progress is kept independent of their handwriting progress. The reading lesson can proceed regardless of the children's handwriting abilities.

Some suggestions for the most effective use of the Level D workbook:

1. Do not ask the children to do the work in a given section of the workbook until they have become acquainted with the sound-spelling patterns used in that section. You may want to begin each section of the workbook by reading the word charts for that section with the children. Have the children read up and down the columns and across the rows, and discuss any unfamiliar words with them before proceeding to the exercises.

2. Throughout the first section of Level D, take care to see that each child understands the directions and is following them correctly before encouraging them to proceed on their own.

3. If a child does not recognize a pictured object, simply tell them what it is.

4. Whenever possible, correct the children's work with them, reading the words, phrases, and sentences aloud and discussing the pictures. The more the children *hear* the words while looking at them, the greater will be their chance to develop automatic word recognition.

5. Try to assess the reasons for the children's errors and deal with them appropriately. Sometimes, as on the riddle pages, an error may be caused by faulty reasoning rather than by faulty decoding. At this stage, accurate decoding is a more important goal than perfect reasoning, and a child who decodes correctly but reasons poorly should still be praised for their reading.

6. Note that the "Yes or No" exercises on pages 8, 23, and 86 are purposely written without clear-cut yes or no answers to every item. These pages should be discussed but not corrected. Make it a general rule *for all formats* not to put undue stress on getting the right answer. Instead, put the stress on accurate decoding and the enjoyment of using reading skills in a problem-solving situation.

Copyright © 2024, 2000, 1985, 1976, 1970, 1965, 1964 by the Estates of Donald E. Rasmussen and Lenina Goldberg. All rights reserved. Except as permitted under the United States Copyright Act, no part of this publication may be reproduced or distributed in any form or by any means, or stored in a database or retrieval system, without prior written permission from the publisher.

Email all inquiries to:
Peter Rasmussen, Editor
info@BasicReading.com

Website: BasicReading.com
ISBN 978-1-937547-04-2

_a_	_e_	_i_	_o_	_u_
bang				
gang				
hang				hung
		king		
				lung
rang		ring		rung
sang		sing		sung
		wing		
		bring		
clang		cling		clung
		fling		flung
		sling		slung
		sting		stung
		swing		swung

1

1

2

3

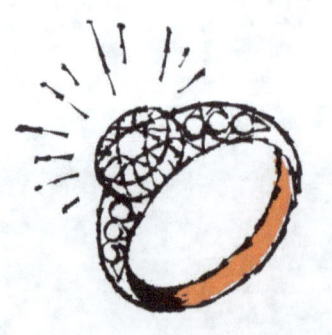
4

a ring   4

a wing

a king

a gang

a swing

to sing

to fling

to clang

5

6

7

8

1

☒ a ring in a tub
☐ a wing on a jet

☐ the bug's sting
☐ the bug's swing

☐ the duck's wings
☐ the gang's rings

☐ a spot to bang
☐ a sled to bring

☐ The swing is singing.
☐ The swing is swinging.

☐ The king is hunting.
☐ The king is resting.

What brings it to my sill?
- ☐ jumping from a stick
- ☒ flapping its wings

What could you hang from it?
- ☐ a swing for the gang
- ☐ a ring for a king

What did it do to Jack?
- ☐ It sang to him.
- ☐ It stung him.

What is it for?
- ☐ banging in some pegs
- ☐ bringing in a snack

1

1

2

3

4

5

6

7

8

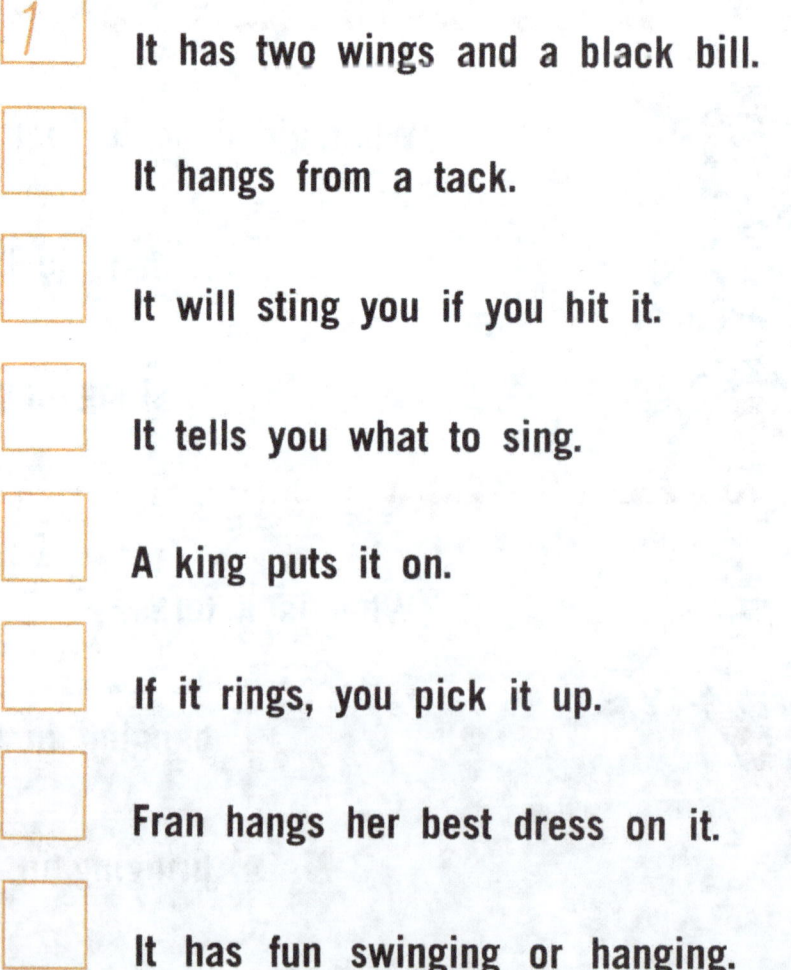

[1] It has two wings and a black bill.

[ ] It hangs from a tack.

[ ] It will sting you if you hit it.

[ ] It tells you what to sing.

[ ] A king puts it on.

[ ] If it rings, you pick it up.

[ ] Fran hangs her best dress on it.

[ ] It has fun swinging or hanging.

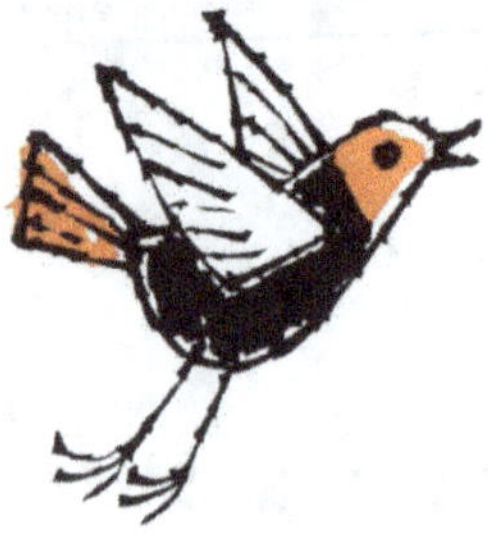

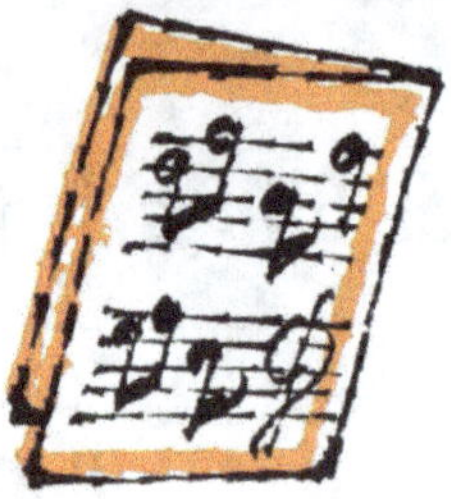

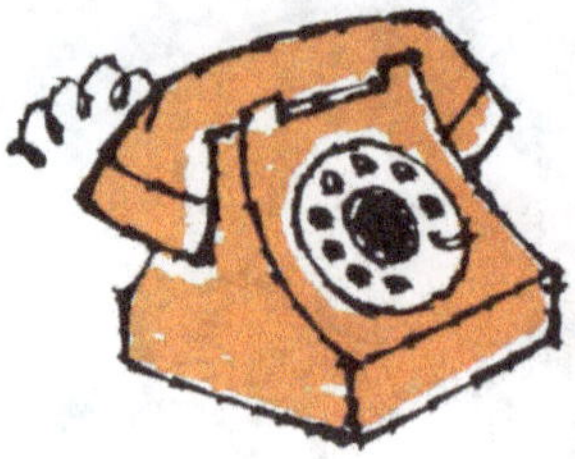

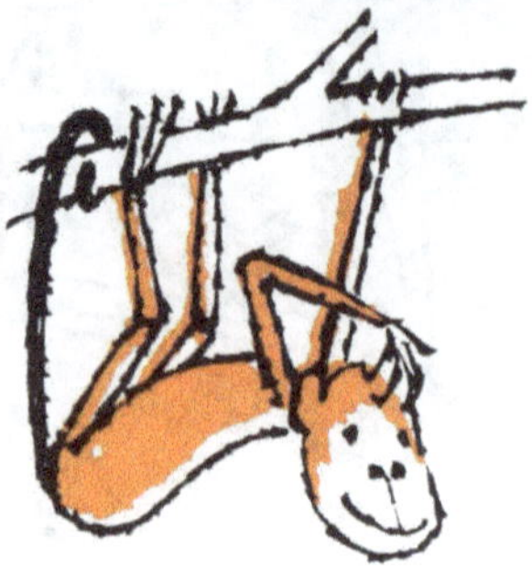

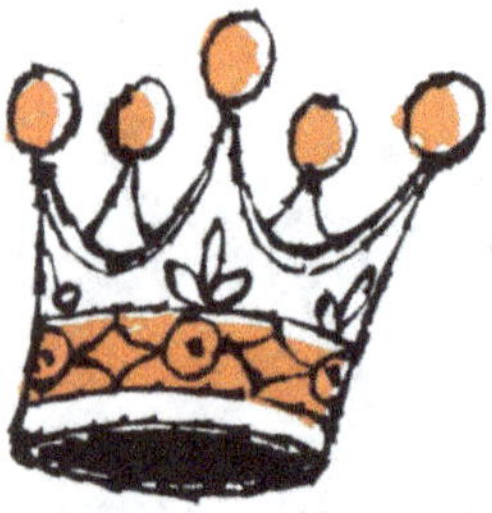

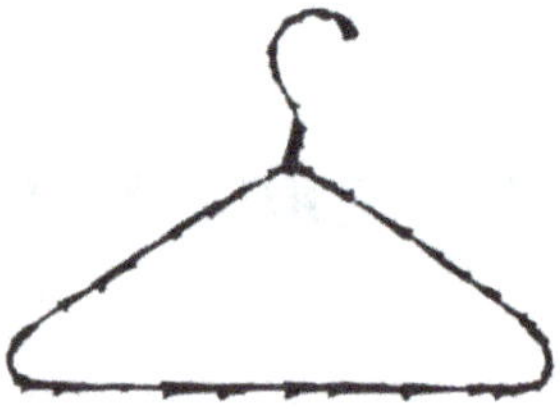

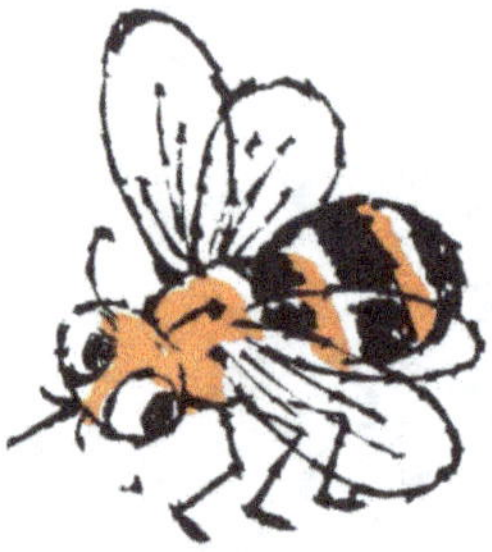

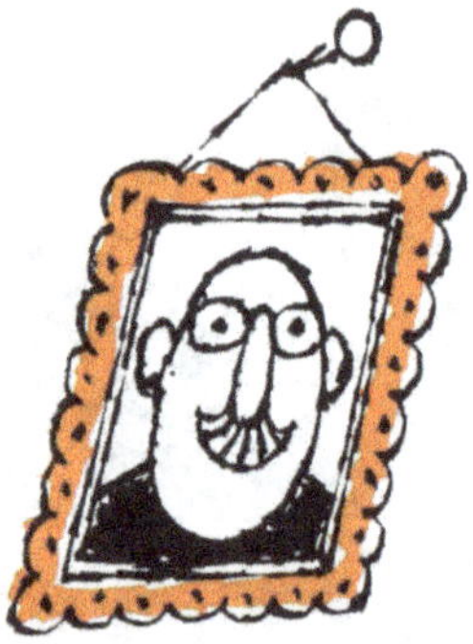

1

She is (hanging) up the dress.
banging

The pals were swimming.
swinging.

Dad hung up his hat.
rang

Puss is singing in the well.
stinging

Yes or No?

It can ring,

but can it sing?

Yes____   No____

You can cling to it,

but can you swing on it?

Yes____   No____

It can sting,

but can it sing?

Yes____   No____

It can bang,

but can it clang?

Yes____   No____

The twins are
- [ ] banging on the drums.
- [ ] bringing in the swing.

The jet's wings are
- [ ] dripping-wet.
- [ ] hunting a pet.

Mom is
- [ ] pressing her dress.
- [ ] dressing her doll.

The gang is
- [ ] stepping up to get the gas.
- [ ] jumping and skipping in the grass.

1

1

2

3

4

☐ Bill said, "Mom is hanging up my socks.
They will swing in the wind."

☐ The class is clapping.
Miss Hill has just said, "You can go swimming."

☐ Fran is bringing her sack to Mom.
She is yelling, "I am going camping."

☐ Tom is running.
He yells, "I am bringing a gift to Ann."

A hen was sitting on an egg.
The hen said, "My egg is

stinging."   cracking."   melting."

The clock's bell won't stop

winging.   ringing.   resting.

The twins said, "Bring your sled for some

swinging."   batting."   sledding."

She is running to pick it up so it will stop

ringing.   banging.   hanging.

1

The gang is going camping.

Dick　　　Fran　　　Jill　　　Jack

	Yes	No
1. The gang is going camping on the hill.	☒	☐
2. Jill is putting up a flag in the camp.	☐	☐
3. They have on black pants and swimming caps.	☐	☐
4. Fran is helping by bringing the milk.	☐	☐
5. Jack is running back to bring the rest of the gang.	☐	☐
6. Dick got stung and is jumping and yelling.	☐	☐
7. Dick is hunting and Jill is digging.	☐	☐

The gang is in the pond.
Stan is telling his pals, "It's fun to go

spilling."   swimming."   singing."

A bug is sitting in Dick's sandbox.
Dick is yelling, "The bug can

stick."   bring."   sting."

A frog is sitting on a rock.
He said, "I don't have any bugs. I must go

hanging."   hunting."   banging."

Jack is still in bed.
His mom is yelling,
"Jack, get up! The bell has

rang."   ring."   rung."

1

Fran has a swing.

	Yes	No
1. Fran's dad has put up a swing for her.	☐	☐
2. The swing is hanging from a brick.	☐	☐
3. Fran is swinging her legs up.	☐	☐
4. Dad is sitting and resting as Fran is swinging.	☐	☐
5. The swing is getting stuck in the grass.	☐	☐
6. Fran is clinging to the swing.	☐	☐
7. As Dad was resting, a bug stung him.	☐	☐

Dad hung it up.

The gang had lots of fun on it.

It isn't for running and jumping.

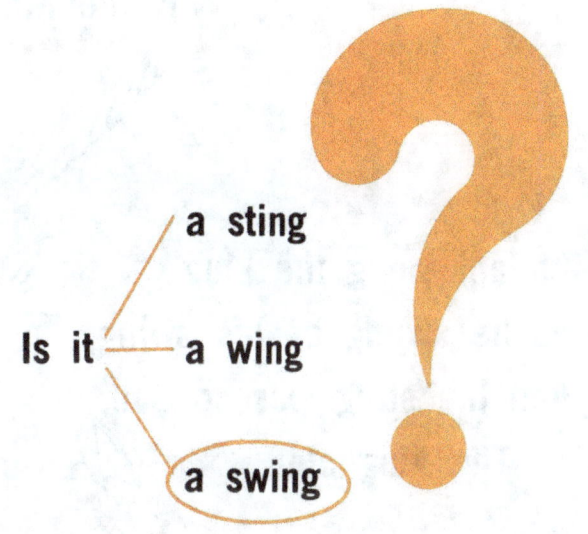

Is it
- a sting
- a wing
- (a swing)

Some clocks do it!

A tub can have it.

A mom can have it on her left hand.

Is it
- a wing
- a ring
- a rung

He can go hunting.

His men come running when he claps his hands.

He has a big ring.

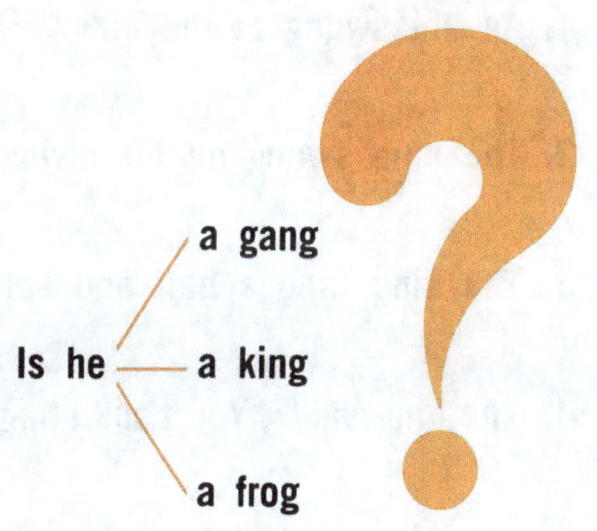

Is he
- a gang
- a king
- a frog

1 Why the King Went to Bed

An ant stung the king
As he swung on his swing,
And the sting was so bad,
   The king bled.

  "Stop the swing!" said the king,
  "I'm so sick from the sting,
  I can't stand it—
     I'm going to bed!"

	Yes	No
1. An ant swung at the king.		☒
2. The king swung on his swing.		
3. The king rang a bell and sang.		
4. The king said, "You can't sting a king!"		
5. The king said, "Stop the swing!"		

_a_	_e_	_i_	_o_	_u_
bank				bunk
				dunk
Hank				hunk
				junk
		pink		
rank		rink		
sank		sink		sunk
tank				
		wink		
yank				
blank		blink		
clank		clink		clunk
plank				
		slink		
				skunk
				spunk
crank				
drank		drink		drunk
Frank				
				trunk

17

☐ to sink
☐ to sing

☐ the elf
☐ the ink

☐ the skunk
☐ the swing

☐ the bunk
☐ the bank

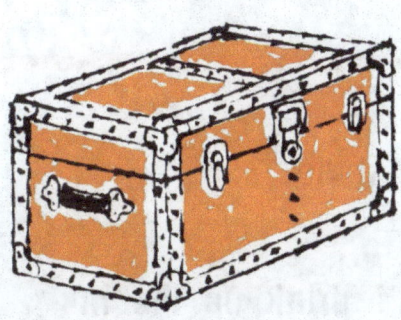

☐ the trunk
☐ the truck

☐ the rink
☐ the ring

2

What would it do?

☐ blink in the sun

☐ sing to a truck

What would it have?

☐ a clanking trunk

☐ a swinging trunk

What can it do?

☐ slink in the grass

☐ get a glass

What will it do?

☐ drink up the ink

☐ bring back a stick

- [ ] We drink it from a big glass.
- [ ] They clink and clank in the sink.
- [ ] He swings his big trunk.
- [ ] You put them on to have fun in a rink.
- [ ] You can drop them in the slot of a bank.
- [ ] If you spill ink on it, Dad will yell.
- [ ] It can wink and blink.
- [ ] It sank in the pond as Frank swam to it.

2

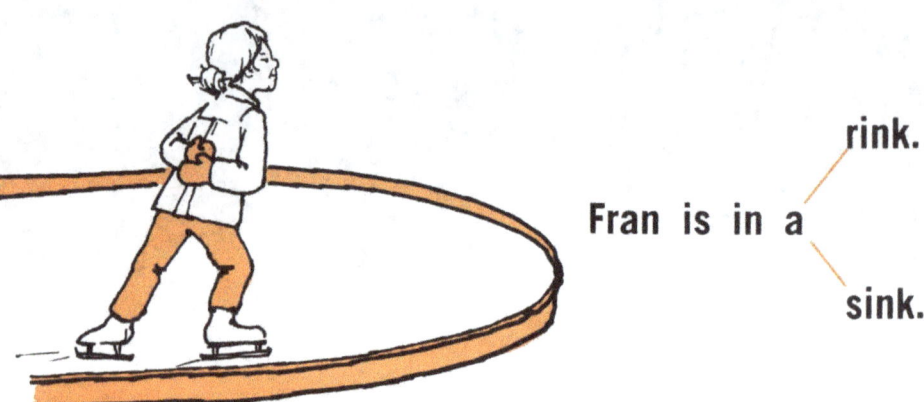

Fran is in a rink. / sink.

The sun is blinking. / sinking.

Frank is drinking milk. / bringing silk.

The skunk sank into the mud. / spanks his pal, Spud.

Yes or No?

A frog can blink

but can it sink?

Yes____ No____

A skunk can yank,

but can it drink?

Yes____ No____

Cans can clank,

but can they blink?

Yes____ No____

Hank can drink,

but can he wink?

Yes____ No____

Fran and Hank are

 going to a rink.

 yanking on a ring.

Mom will

 fix the sink.

 get a wink.

Frank

 drinks milk as he sits in his bunk.

 drinks milk as he sits in the sink.

The skunk

 packs a bag and gets a trunk.

 fell into a box of junk.

1

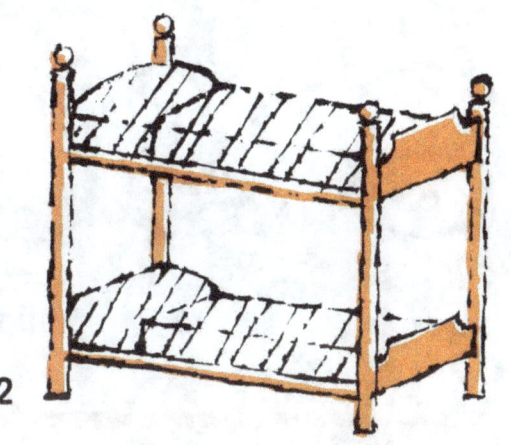
2

3

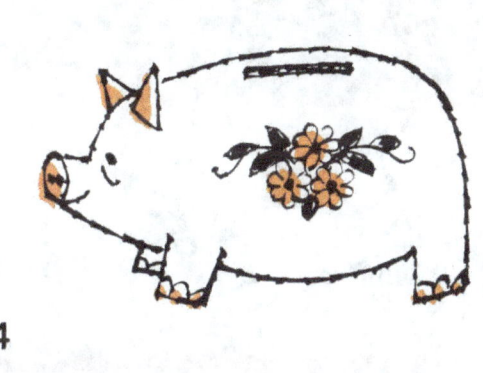
4

☐ Dad said to Mom, "The cup is so hot, I can't drink from it."

☐ Hank said, "Clink! Clank! I can tell my pig bank is filling up."

☐ Fran said, "My dolls must nap. I will put them in the bunk beds."

☐ Hank yelled "No, no!" to his pet skunk. "You can't yank the can of junk."

2

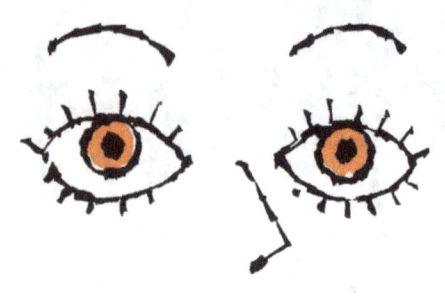

If some sand gets in them, they'll

blink.　　　　blank.　　　　clink.

She won't be glad if you upset the

wink.　　　　ink.　　　　link.

If you drag it, it will

cling.　　　　spank.　　　　clank.

Frank said, "The two cats are still

slinking."　　　　blinking."　　　　drinking."

The twins—Hank and Fran

	Yes	No
1. Hank and Fran have bunk beds.	☐	☐
2. A trunk is next to Fran's bunk.	☐	☐
3. Hank is in the top bunk.	☐	☐
4. Fran lets her left leg hang from the bed.	☐	☐
5. Fran is getting Hank a drink.	☐	☐
6. The twins have some skunks in the trunk.	☐	☐
7. The twins are swinging.	☐	☐

Frank has put his raft in the pond.
He is asking, "Why is it

slinking?"   sinking?"   swinging?"

Jill Franks has a pet.
She is yelling to Mom,
"I have a snack for my

spank."   swing."   skunk."

The sun is setting in the west.
Fred asks his dad, "Do I have to go to bed?"

"It would be best," said Dad.
"You've got to get

nest."   rest."   test."

Frank yells, "A frog is jumping from the bank into the pond."

Fran yells back, "Yes, the frog can dunk itself in the pond, but it won't

sunk."   sink."   swing."

Milk to drink

	Yes	No
1. Mrs. Frank brings the milk for Ann to drink.	☐	☐
2. Muff is napping on the rug.	☐	☐
3. Fran is doing her spelling at the desk.	☐	☐
4. Ann is helping Mom at the sink.	☐	☐
5. Hank is sitting on two pink eggs in a nest.	☐	☐
6. Fran has some ink and a pen on her desk.	☐	☐
7. Hank is yanking Muff's left leg.	☐	☐

You can get it in a glass.

You can get it at the sink.

2 If you spill it, you will have a mess.

Is it
- a blink
- a drink
- a spank

It can be sent to camp.

Dad can pack belts and pants in it.

It is a help on a trip.

Is it
- a tank
- a sting
- a trunk

If it fell, it could crack.

It has a slot in it.

Frank can get a gift if it has a lot in it.

Is it
- a bank
- a bang
- a blank

The Junkman's Skunk

The junkman's skunk will sit and beg
For nuts and snacks and drinks,
And if the junkman picks her up,
She nods at him and winks.

She's kept in a pen on the junkman's truck,
And she drinks from a pink tin cup,
Her bed is just a big flat plank
The junkman has put up.

The junkman lets me pet his skunk
And fix her snacks and drinks,
But she won't nod or wink at ME:
She just sits still and blinks.

	Yes	No
1. The junkman's skunk begs for nods and winks.	☐	☒
2. The junkman's skunk drinks from a pink tin plank.	☐	☐
3. The junkman's skunk sits still and blinks at ME.	☐	☐
4. The skunk will sit and beg for nuts and snacks and drinks.	☐	☐
5. The junkman will not let me pet his skunk. He said she would snap at my leg.	☐	☐

3

_a_	_e_	_i_	_o_	_u_
		ship	shop	
			shot	shut
	shed			
shall	shell			
	shelf			
		shift		
shack			shock	

_a_	_e_	_i_	_o_	_u_
ash				
cash				
dash		dish		
		fish		
				hush
				mush
rash				rush
sash				
		wish		
				blush
flash	flesh			flush
slash			slosh	slush
smash				
				brush
crash				crush
	fresh			
trash				

3

1

2

3

4

a shed

a ship

to shop □

a shelf □

to crash

a dish □

a fish □

a brush □

5

6

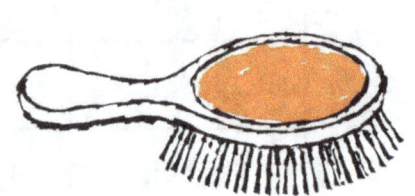
7

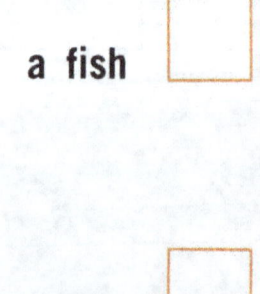

8

1

2

3

4

a trash can

eggshells

a shopping bag

a frog

a wishing well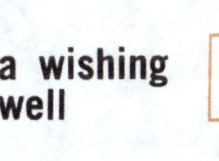

a big rash

a fish tank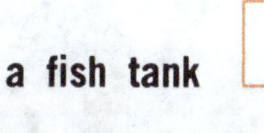

a dishpan

5

6

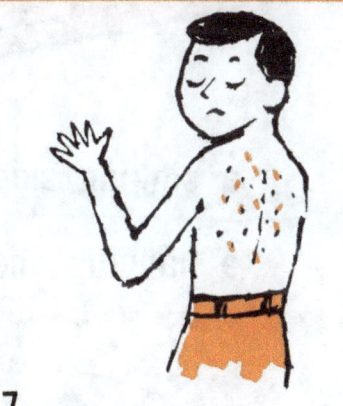
7

8

3

35

3

☐ Hank's fishing
☐ Frank's wishing

☐ Mom's rushing.
☐ Mom's blushing.

☐ a sinking ship
☐ a hanging shelf

☐ a fresh fish
☐ a flashing ring

☐ Mom in the slush
☐ Mom has a brush.

☐ Frank must hush.
☐ Frank must dash.

There is
- ☐ a can of trash.
- ☐ a doll in a trunk.

Frank has
- ☐ a skunk in a shed.
- ☐ a ship in a sink.

There is
- ☐ a flash in the sky.
- ☐ a sash on a fly.

There is
- ☐ a fish rushing by.
- ☐ a dish crashing by.

- [ ] Two fish can have fun swimming in it.
- [ ] Bess is putting a sash on her dress.
- [ ] He is resting on a swing in a pet shop.
- [ ] Dad puts trash and junk into it.
- [ ] You can put some into a dish for the cat to drink.
- [ ] If you want it, you'll have to smash the shell.
- [ ] Fran has a brush to dip into it.
- [ ] Fred can slam it shut.

The trash can by the shed is shot. / shut.

3

The jet is brushing / rushing up into the sky.

The ship is frying / trying to dock.

Mom is trying to fit the dish on the shell. / shelf.

Yes or No?

A ship can crash,

    but can it mash?

Yes____   No____

Miss Cash can fish,

but can she wish?

Yes____   No____

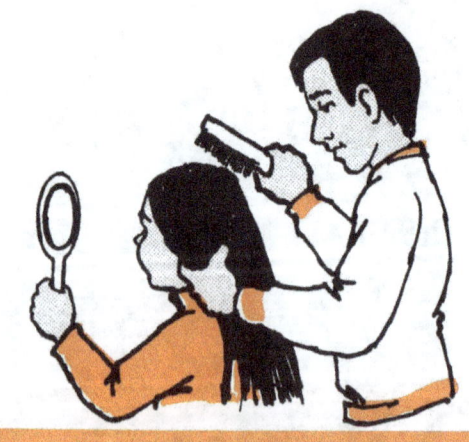

Dad can brush,

but can he rush?

Yes____   No____

A dish can crash,

    but can it flash?

Yes____   No____

What will she do for you?

☐ fix your dish

☐ let you have a wish

3

What can Ann dip into it?

☐ a flat brush

☐ a pink bank

What can you put in here?

☐ some fresh fish

☐ some junk and trash

Why would he come?

☐ to smash my dolls

☐ to help me get rid of my rash

3

1

2

3

4

☐ Mom was mixing the eggs.
She said, "I must not let the shells drop into the eggs."

☐ Bill felt a tug on his fishing rod.
Bill said, "It must be a fish!"

☐ Bill held up his fish.
He said, "I wish I had a lot of fresh fish for Mom to fry."

☐ The box on the shelf was shut.
Mom said, "I wish I could lift the lid on this box."

Mom is putting a fish on a

dish.　　　ship.　　　hush.

3

The skunk is tipping the trash can. The can will go

slush.　　　cash.　　　crash.

Spot is rushing into the dress

stop.　　　ship.　　　shop.

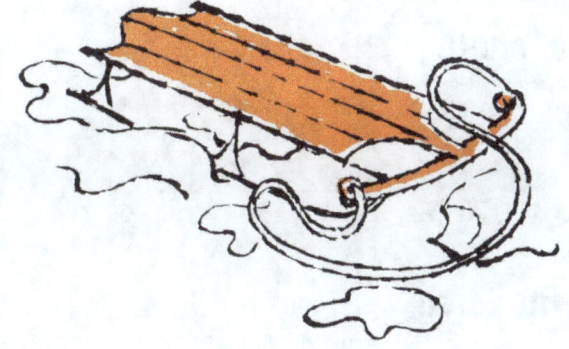

Sledding is not fun in the

shift.　　　slash.　　　slush.

43

Fran has a pet.

	Yes	No
1. Fran is ringing the bell so her cat will come in.	☐	☐
2. Puff is rushing off. He won't come in.	☐	☐
3. Puff is dashing to Fran.	☐	☐
4. Fran is putting fresh milk in Puff's dish.	☐	☐
5. Fran is putting Puff's fresh milk on a shelf.	☐	☐
6. Puff is smashing the dish of milk.	☐	☐
7. Puff is drinking the fresh milk from the dish.	☐	☐

Frank was sitting in the sand. He said, "It's lots of fun digging with my

ship."   shed."   shell."

Lill said, "I can't get into the shed. I didn't know it was

shut."   shot."   hut."

Beth said to Mom, "I cannot get the trunk in the shed."

Mom said, "It isn't in the shed, it's on Dad's

self."   shift."   shelf."

Frank said, "I must rush and pack my trunk. I am going on a trip on a

shop."   ship."   sink."

3

It will smash if you drop it.

Mom puts it on a shelf.

Cats wish Mom would put milk in it.

Is it
- a fish
- a dash
- a dish

It can swim past in a flash.

Dad sits wishing he could get it.

Mom can fry it if it is fresh.

Is it
- a dish
- a flash
- a fish

A duck or a hen can come from it.

If you step on it, you will smash it.

If you crush it, you cannot fix it.

Is it
- a shall
- a shell
- a shelf

Said a Duck

Said a duck, just cracking her shell,
"I wish I could fly for a spell!"
    She went FLAP! She went DASH!
    She DID try, but went crash.
"What a shock!" said the duck as she fell.

        Said the duck, rushing off to the pond,
        "Of swimming I'll try to be fond.
           If I'm wet, I shan't cry,
           For I know I'm drip-dry,
      So I'll slosh and I'll swish in the pond."

	Yes	No
1. The duck said, "I wish I could cry for a spell."	☐	☐
2. "What a shell!" said the duck as she fell.	☐	☐
3. The duck said she would try to be fond of swimming.	☐	☐
4. The duck said, "I know I can fly, so I'll flap up to the sky."	☐	☐
5. The duck said, "I know I'm drip-dry, so I'll slosh and I'll swish in the pond."	☐	☐

_a_	_e_	_i_	_o_	_u_
		thin		
thank		think		
		thing		
		thick		
				thump
bath	Beth			
	tenth			
path				
		with		
		Smith		
		fifth		
		sixth		

What are the hens doing?

☐ The ten hens run up the path.

☐ The fifth hen flaps her wings.

What is Mr. Smith doing?

☐ Mr. Smith sits on a thick rug.

☐ Mr. Smith sits and thinks.

What is Beth getting?

☐ Beth gets something for a snack.

☐ Beth gets a thin stick from the shelf.

What did Beth get?

☐ Beth got a ring from Mr. Smith.

☐ Beth got a bathtub for her mom.

1 2 3 4

5 6 7 8

☐ This is fun in a bathtub or a pond.

☐ This is something Beth must brush.

☐ This fits on top of a trash can.

☐ This is something to thump on.

☐ This has a thin shell to crack.

☐ This is something for fishing.

☐ This is what I want to have with milk.

☐ This is something that helps Beth to swim.

This thing is
- thin.
- thick.

Beth can
- thump on it.
- think on it.

The skunk
- ran on the path.
- fell into the bath.

This is
- something for fishing.
- something for singing.

Yes or No?

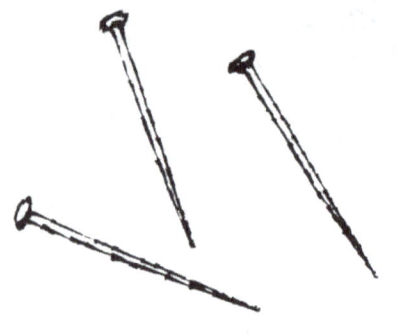

A pin is thin,

    but can it spin?

        Yes____   No____

Beth can run up a path,

    but can she run in a bath?

        Yes____   No____

A drum is something to thump on,

    but is it something to jump on?

        Yes____   No____

A clock is something that ticks,

    but can you set it at six?

        Yes____   No____

What is that on his back?

☐ a thin shed

☐ a thick shell

What is the fifth man doing?

☐ drinking milk

☐ thinking of something

What is in back of them?

☐ thin glass

☐ thick grass

What can we dip into this?

☐ a wet bath

☐ a thin brush

☐ Something sat on Mr. Smith's hand.
Mr. Smith said, "What's that?"

☐ Bill had a snack for Mr. and Mrs. Banks.
But they said, "No thank you, Bill. We don't want anything."

☐ Mr. Hill got the brick in on his tenth try.
He said, "This is the last brick for the path."

☐ Beth got something for Mrs. Banks.
She said, "I think you'll want this, Mrs. Banks."

Hank was drinking lots of milk.
He said, "This glass is my

with."   fifth."   tenth."

4

Beth said, "What is in this glass?"
Hank said, "It's pop to drink."
Beth said,

"Things."   "Thumps."   "Thanks."

Bill said, "The fish are so thin."
Ben said, "But I just fed

them."   than."   then."

Ned's Mom was mad. She began to yell,
"Ned, get rid of the frogs in my

bathtub!"   path!"   Beth!"

Yes or No?

A cat can drink,
but can it think?

Yes____ No____

4

A trash can can clank,
but can it thank?

Yes____ No____

Fish can swim in a tank,
but can they swim in a thank?

Yes____ No____

You can have a brick path,
but can you have a brick bath?

Yes____ No____

Beth and Jill have fun.

Beth   Jill

	Yes	No
1. Beth and Jill are resting on a path.	☐	☐
2. Beth is digging for something in the sand.	☐	☐
3. Jill is sitting and thinking.	☐	☐
4. Jill is thumping a drum with her hand.	☐	☐
5. Beth is dashing in for a swim with Jill.	☐	☐
6. Jill has on a thin cap for swimming.	☐	☐
7. Beth has something in her hand.	☐	☐

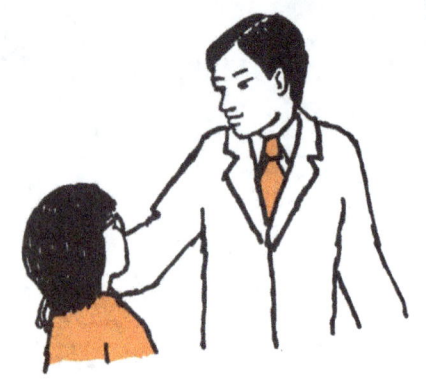

Dad said to Beth, "At ten I have to go shopping. Will you come with me

then?"   that?"   this?"

Beth went with her dad.
Dad said, "We'll go in this shop and get

swinging."   something."   swimming."

Dad had a gift for Beth.
Beth ran to him and said,

"Anything."   "Think you."   "Thank you."

"What do you have, Beth?" said Mrs. Hill.
Beth said, "I have two of

then."   them."   tenth."

Ms. Smith has a pet shop.

	Yes	No
1. Six fish are swimming in the tank.	☐	☐
2. Ms. Smith's fish swim in this tank.	☐	☐
3. Ms. Smith is putting fresh shells in the tank.	☐	☐
4. The fish must be fed so that they won't be thin.	☐	☐
5. Ms. Smith thinks the fish should be fed.	☐	☐
6. Some of the fish have thin spots on them.	☐	☐
7. The fish ask Ms. Smith if they can do anything for her.	☐	☐

You can bang it with a stick.

You can thump it with your hand.

A band can have many of them.

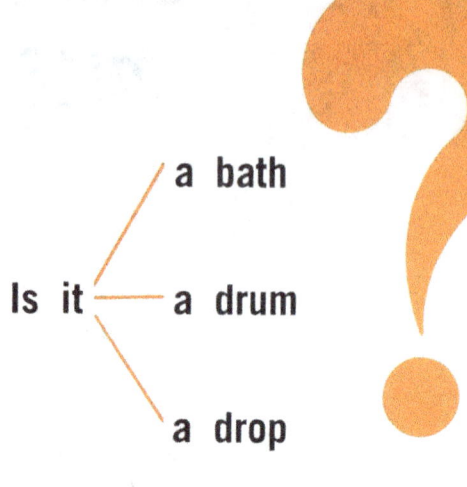
Is it a bath, a drum, a drop?

4

You can sit in it.

You can put suds in it.

You can get wet in it.

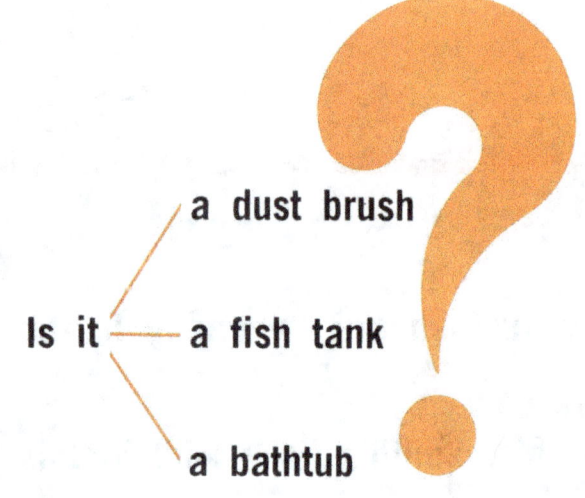
Is it a dust brush, a fish tank, a bathtub?

It is thin and can crack if it drops.

It fits on a shelf.

The sink is its bathtub.

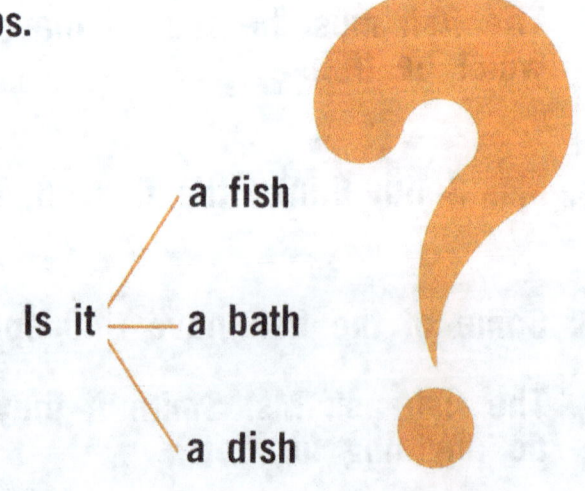
Is it a fish, a bath, a dish?

I Think I'll Be

I think I'll be a fish
    That can swim in a dish.
Or should I be a bug,
    With a nest in a rug?
I think I'll be an elf
    Not as big as myself.
Or I could be a king
    Who can do just anything!
I think I'll be a frog,
    And thump on a log.
And the sixth thing I'll be?
    Why—I think I'll be ME!

	Yes	No
1. I think I'll be a fish that can swim in a dishrag.	☐	☐
2. I think I'll be a frog and thump on a log.	☐	☐
3. I think I'll be a bug with a nest in a brush.	☐	☐
4. I think I'll be a king not as big as an elf.	☐	☐
5. I think I'll be an elf not as big as myself.	☐	☐

_a_	_e_	_i_	_o_	_u_
				chug
				chum
		chin		
chap		chip	chop	
chat	Chet			
	check	chick		Chuck
		chill		
	chest			
				much
		rich		
				such
		inch		
	bench			bunch
				lunch
		pinch		punch
ranch				

5

☐ a bunch
☐ a lunch

☐ a bunch
☐ a bench

☐ a pinch
☐ a punch

☐ a hunch
☐ a lunch

☐ a chip
☐ a chap

☐ an inch
☐ a pinch

There is

☐ rich Miss Bunch.

☐ a chap at lunch.

Dad is

☐ chopping for lunch.

☐ shopping for lunch.

5

Brad and Beth and Ann get

☐ a wet bunch.

☐ a hot lunch.

The gang has

☐ much fun.

☐ such sun.

67

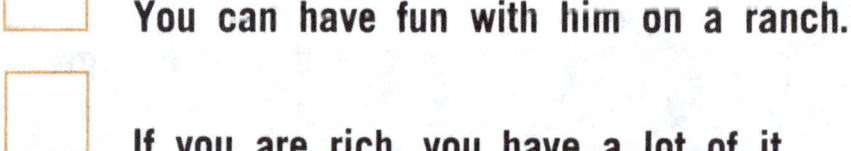

☐ You can have fun with him on a ranch.

☐ If you are rich, you have a lot of it.

☐ Chuck can chin himself.

☐ Dad can sit on it or he can chop it.

☐ It fits into Father's lunch box, and he drinks from it.

☐ A bunch of them will fill a dish.

☐ You can punch it with your fist.

☐ If you pinch it, it will pop.

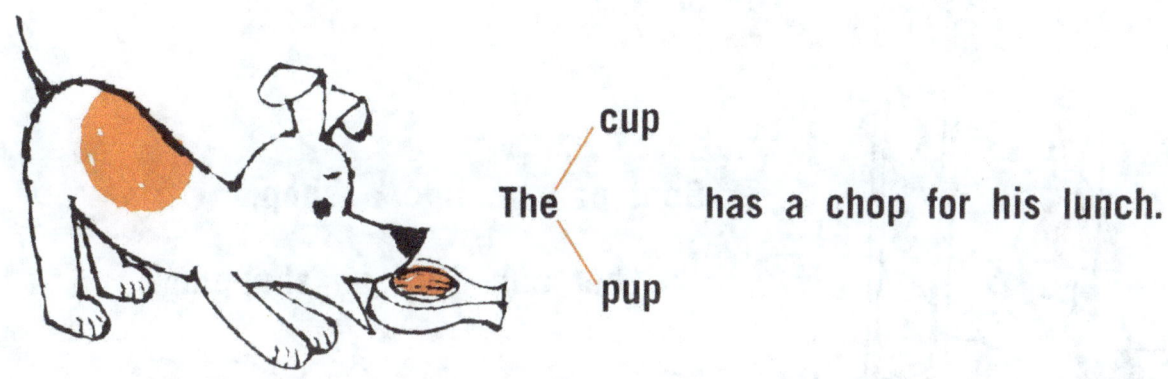

The cup / pup has a chop for his lunch.

Jim's father is checking his list. / fist.

Mrs. Smith has a sandwich for her lunch. / some punch for lunch.

Another brother is sitting on the bench. / on the bunch.

Yes or No?

Spot can go into a shop,

but can Spot go shopping?

Yes____   No____

A crab can pinch,

but can he get rich?

Yes____   No____

A chip can fly,

but can it cry?

Yes____   No____

A bench has legs,

but can it run?

Yes____   No____

What would you put next to the bed?

☐ a chest and a bench

☐ a lunch box and a chop

What is she doing?

☐ She is checking up on Bill.

☐ She is running to get her chicks.

Where will it go?

☐ It will hop into a chest.

☐ It will hop up on the bench.

What is she doing?

☐ She is chilling the punch for lunch.

☐ She is chopping the eggs for lunch.

5

1

2

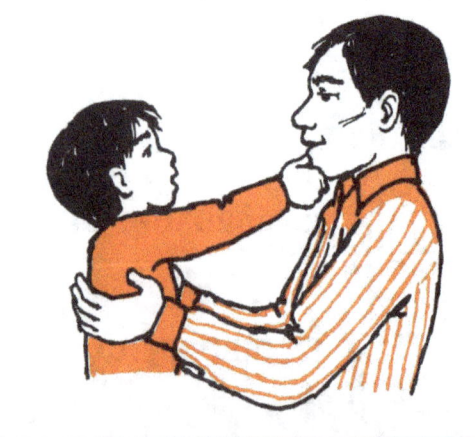
3

4

☐ Mother said, "I'll put a fresh sandwich in my lunch box."

☐ Mother said, "I must check this map so I can get to Mr. Smith's shop."

☐ Brad said, "I'm glad Chuck is my chum."
Chuck said, "I'm glad Brad is my best pal."

☐ Father said, "I think Ned is trying to pinch my chin."

If you have so much of it, you are

inch.   rich.   such.

If a glass of milk drips on you, you must dry your

chin.   chip.   chop.

If you have one, you can fix yourself a ham

sandwich.   sandbag.   sandbox.

If you get wet and stand in the wind, you can get a

pill.   chill.   shell.

5

Beth's brother

5

	Yes	No
1. Beth and her brother are having fish for lunch.	☐	☐
2. Beth will have punch and a sandwich for lunch.	☐	☐
3. Beth is sitting on a bench, and her brother is on a chest.	☐	☐
4. Beth's sandwich is as thick as her brother's.	☐	☐
5. Beth is telling her father to sit on the bench with her.	☐	☐
6. Beth and her brother have some chopsticks — just for fun.	☐	☐
7. Beth's brother was drinking the punch so fast that he got some on his chin.	☐	☐

Father had his lunch box.
He said, "I will sit on this bench and have my

bunch."   lung."   lunch."

Father was dishing up lunch.
Father said, "Do you want a

chat?"   chop?"   check?"

Mom was fixing lunch.
She said, "Do you want a sandwich and

punch?"   bunch?"   bench?"

The chick ran up to the nut.
She said, "Mother Hen! Can I have a nut for my

bench?"   lunch?"   link?"

Chuck's chums

5

	Yes	No
1. Chuck and his chums are on a ranch in the West.	☐	☐
2. Chuck has an ax and is chopping a log.	☐	☐
3. The chips are flying as Beth chops a log.	☐	☐
4. Chuck's other chums are shopping.	☐	☐
5. Some logs are lying in a stack.	☐	☐
6. Some of Chuck's chums are sitting on a bench and are not doing much to help Chuck.	☐	☐
7. The chum on the bench is spinning a top.	☐	☐

It comes from one egg.

You can have such fun with it!

Its mother is a hen.

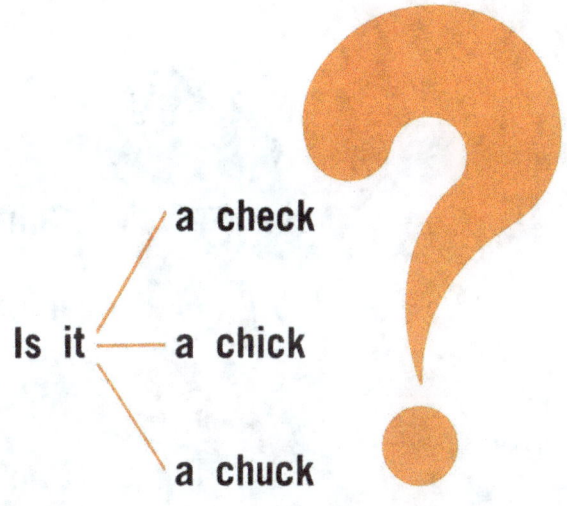

Is it — a check
— a chick
— a chuck

You can drink it.

You can spill it.

You can chill it.

Is it — bunch
— punch
— pinch

You can't chop it, chip it, or chill it.

You can't pinch it or punch it.

It is not thick.

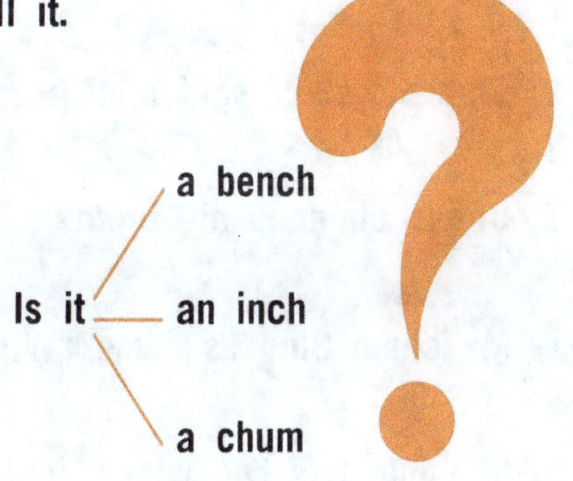

Is it — a bench
— an inch
— a chum

5

Chip Is My Chum

Chip is my chum. He asks me why
A fish can swim, but cannot fly.
And why a bug that has two wings
Can fly but can't do other things.

He asks so much, I want to cry,
"Why must you ask me WHY, WHY, WHY?"
Chip's my chum. Yes, he's my brother.
Another "Why?" and I'll ask Mother.

	Yes	No
1. If a fish can swim, it can fly.	☐	☐
2. Chip's brother said a dish can fly.	☐	☐
3. Chip's chum is his brother, not his mother.	☐	☐
4. My chum Chip asks me "WHY, WHY, WHY?"	☐	☐
5. If a bug has two wings, it can cry.	☐	☐

_a_	_e_	_i_	_o_	_u_
		itch		
catch				
		ditch		Dutch
hatch		hitch		
latch				
match		Mitch		
patch		pitch		
		witch		
				clutch
				crutch
snatch				
		stitch		
		switch		

_a_	_e_	_i_	_o_	_u_
whack		whim		
wham				
	when			
		which		
		whiff		
		whip		
		whisk		
		quit		
		quiz		
		quilt		
quack		quick		

☐ a chick
☐ a crutch

☐ a quilt
☐ a quiz

☐ to pinch
☐ to pitch

☐ to chop
☐ to catch

☐ a whip
☐ a ship

☐ to crush
☐ to catch

What does she have?

☐ She has a patch.

☐ She has a crutch.

What is she doing?

☐ She is catching.

☐ She is pitching.

What is going on?

☐ The elf is catching.

☐ The eggs are hatching.

What is she doing?

☐ She is putting a match to it.

☐ She is putting a patch on it.

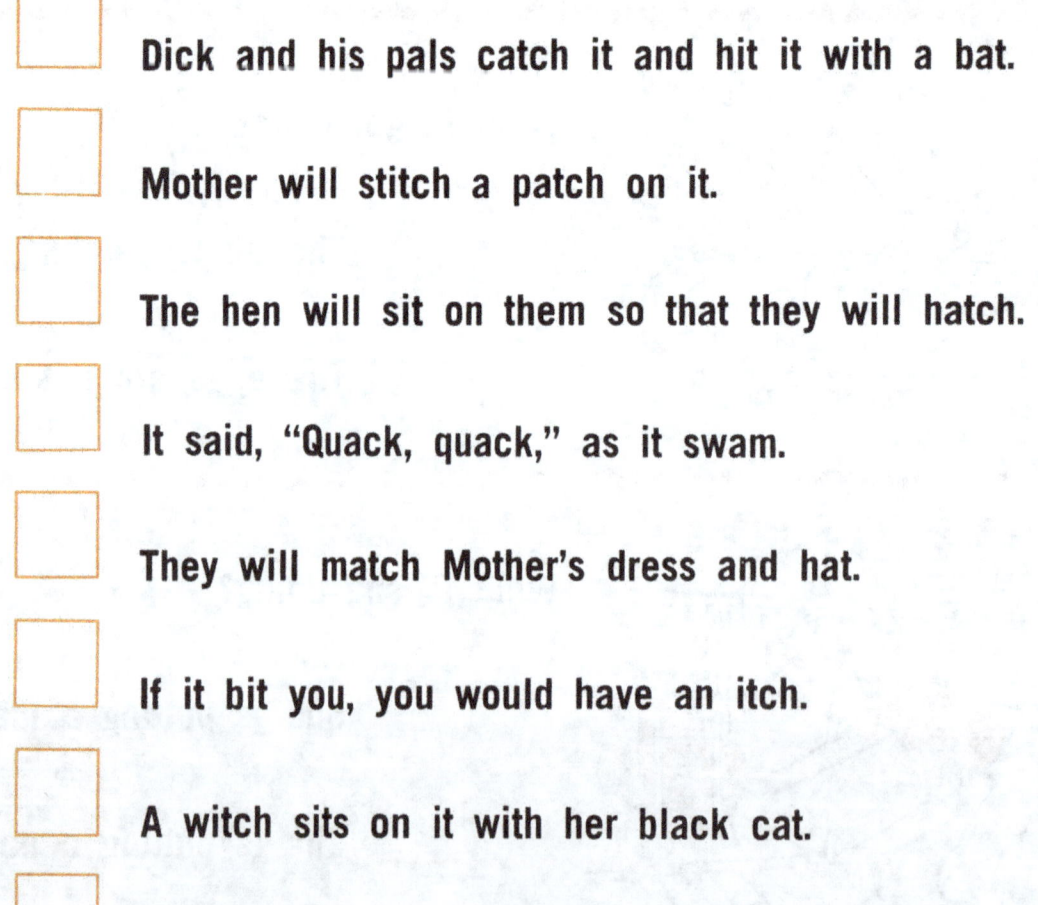

☐ Dick and his pals catch it and hit it with a bat.

☐ Mother will stitch a patch on it.

☐ The hen will sit on them so that they will hatch.

☐ It said, "Quack, quack," as it swam.

☐ They will match Mother's dress and hat.

☐ If it bit you, you would have an itch.

☐ A witch sits on it with her black cat.

☐ Mother lit it with a match.

Mitch wants to pass the { quick quiz. / quick quilt. }

The duck can { quack / crack } as it runs.

Dad is running to { cash his checks. / catch his chicks. }

The { witch / match } is in the { ditch. / dish. }

Yes or No?

Bess can swing,

but can she sing?

Yes____   No____

Hens can hatch,

but can they catch?

Yes____   No____

A duck can quack,

but can it crack?

Yes____   No____

If she can pitch,

can she dig a ditch?

Yes____   No____

What will he do?

☐ He will patch and stitch.

☐ He will pitch and catch.

What can she do?

☐ She can catch her lunch.

☐ She can hatch a bunch.

What will he do?

☐ He will dig a ditch.

☐ He will catch a fish.

What will he do?

☐ He will jump and catch.

☐ He will get a crutch.

1

2

3

4

☐ "Swish, swish," said the witch as she was flying on the quilt.

☐ "I'll catch the bus here," said Frank as he was resting on the bench.

☐ "Quack, quack," said the two ducks as they were swimming on the pond.

☐ "I must rush," said Beth. "I am dressing to pitch and to catch."

The ducks were swimming and

quitting.   quacking.   quilting.

A bug was stinging, and they were

itching.   pitching.   inching.

The mother hen was clucking as the eggs were

brushing.   hushing.   hatching.

One was pitching, and the other was

punching.   catching.   cashing.

What will the witch do?

6

	Yes	No
1. The witch is flying in the sky.	☐	☐
2. The witch has a whip in her hand.	☐	☐
3. The witch is digging in the ditch.	☐	☐
4. The man will fly up to catch the witch.	☐	☐
5. The witch has a patch on her dress.	☐	☐
6. A duck is quacking next to the path.	☐	☐
7. The man is snatching the hat that the witch has on.	☐	☐

The twins were stitching on a quilt.
Dick had to ask, "Which twin is

which?" witch?" wish?"

Ann wasn't well.
She said, "I'll have to

quack." quiz." quit."

Mom and Dad had to patch a quilt.
Dad said, "I'll get another patch.
This one doesn't

match." mash." much."

A fox was going to snatch the eggs
from the nest. The mother duck said,

"Quilt! Quilt!"   "Quick! Quick!"
"Quack! Quack!"

Chet helps his mother.

6

	Yes	No
1. Chet's mother is stitching a patch on a quilt..	☐	☐
2. Chet is handing his mother another patch for the quilt.	☐	☐
3. Chet is stitching a patch on another quilt.	☐	☐
4. A witch is trying to snatch the quilt.	☐	☐
5. Chet's mother is handing him a patch.	☐	☐
6. The quilt has just one patch on it.	☐	☐
7. The quilt is for a bed.	☐	☐

It can be lit.

When it is lit, it is hot.

It is not a toy.

Is it — a match / a witch / a watch

Many of them will mend a rip.

Many of them will patch a quilt.

Many of them can mend the hem in a dress.

Is it — a switch / a pitch / a stitch

It has a black hat and dress.

It can fly into the sky.

It can cast a spell.

Is it — a witch / a switch / a wish

The Clock

I have a big clock
   That sits on a shelf.
When I am not there,
   It just ticks to itself.

But what is it for?
   I don't have to ask.
The clock tells me when
   I should do my next task.

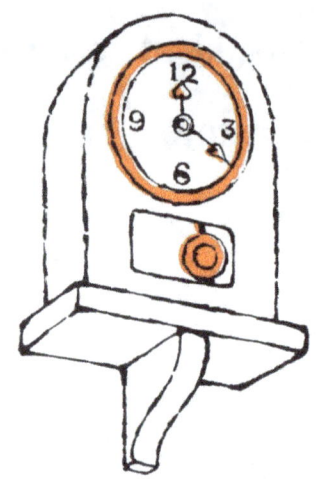

If I have some stitching
   In my mending kit,
I know when to do it,
   And when I must quit.

I have a big clock.
   YOU'D think it went "Tick,"
But to me, with my tasks,
   It's going "Quick! Quick!"

	Yes	No
1. My big clock tells me when I should do my next task.	☐	☐
2. My big clock tells me when to hatch an egg.	☐	☐
3. My big clock sits on a shelf and quacks to itself.	☐	☐
4. My big clock sits on a shelf and ticks to itself.	☐	☐
5. My big clock whacks me and tells me when I should do my next task.	☐	☐

www.ingramcontent.com/pod-product-compliance
Lightning Source LLC
Chambersburg PA
CBHW080444090526
44586CB00047B/2443